THE MAGIC FLUTE

THE STORY
OF
MOZART'S OPERA

Francesca Crespi

retold by Margaret Greaves

Henry Holt and Company · New York

for the St John's Wood Opera Group

First published in Great Britain in 1989
by Methuen Children's Books Ltd

Published in the United States by Henry Holt and Company, Inc.
115 West 18th Street, New York, New York 10011.

Library of Congress Cataloging-in-Publication Data

Crespi, Francesca.
The magic flute: the story of Mozart's opera/[illustrated by] Francesca Crespi;
retold by Margaret Greaves. — 1st American ed.   p.   cm.
Summary: Retells the story of the Mozart opera, in which the noble Prince Tamino
seeks the fair Pamina against a backdrop of the battle between darkness and light.
ISBN 0-8050-0887-X
1. Mozart, Wolfgang Amadeus. 1756–1791. Zauberflöte.
2. Operas—Stories, plots, etc. [1. Operas—Stories, plots, etc.]
I. Greaves, Margaret. II. Mozart, Wolfgang Amadeus, 1756–1791. Zauberflöte. III. Title.
MT100.M765C7   1989
782.1′3—dc19   88-25922

First American edition
Printed in Italy by L.E.G.O.
10 9 8 7 6 5 4 3 2 1

The *Magic Flute* was Mozart's last opera:
it was first performed in Vienna on
September 30th, 1791, two months before his death.
It was a great success and remains one of
the most popular operas to this day.

One day, as Prince Tamino was hunting in an unknown forest, a monstrous serpent suddenly reared up in his path. The poor Prince had run out of arrows and was forced to flee from the hideous creature. He twisted and turned among the trees and thorns and brambles, but still it pursued him until, utterly exhausted, he fainted and fell.

At that very moment three mysterious ladies, darkly veiled and armed with spears, appeared.

"Die, abominable serpent!" they cried.

The serpent fell slain before them. The ladies
looked down at the young man they had rescued.
        "How handsome he is!" they said. "Let us
hurry to tell our Queen. Perhaps he can restore
the peace that she has lost."

The ladies vanished and when Prince Tamino recovered he saw no one but a very odd-looking fellow dressed all in feathers and playing merrily on his pipes.

"Who are you?" asked the astonished Prince.

"I'm Papageno, the bird-catcher. I catch birds for the Queen of Night and her ladies, and they pay me in wine and sweetmeats and fruits."

"Have you ever seen the Queen?"

"The star-blazing Queen in her veil of woven darkness!" exclaimed Papageno. "No human sight can pierce that."

Tamino looked at the dead serpent. "But you, surely, are more than human," he said. "How did you kill the serpent without any weapons?"

"Serpent? What serpent? – Oh! – Oh, I strangled it," boasted Papageno.

Instantly the three ladies reappeared. "Papageno!" they scolded.

"No wine for you today, Papageno. Only water."

"No sweetmeats today, Papageno. Only a stone."

"No fruit today, Papageno. Only this padlock."

And they closed poor Papageno's mouth with a golden padlock so that he could tell no more lies.

"Prince," the ladies said, "it was we who saved you."

Then they gave Tamino a locket containing the picture of a beautiful young girl. "Our Queen sends you this picture of her daughter Pamina. The magician Sarastro has abducted her and keeps her a prisoner in his castle."

Tamino fell instantly in love with the Princess Pamina.

"Let me go to her rescue," he cried. "Tell me where the tyrant lives."

"He lives," said the ladies, "in a sunny valley near our mountains. But his castle is guarded against all comers."

Darkness and thunder followed their words.

"She comes! She comes!" cried the ladies.

Out of a black gloom pierced by brilliant stars the
Queen of Night appeared before the wondering
Prince.

"Have no fear, noble Tamino! You have
heard my sorrow, the loss of my darling child. All
my tears are powerless against the craft of the
sorcerer Sarastro. You alone, Prince, can save her.
Return with her in triumph and she shall be yours
forever."

The trailing clouds of darkness closed round her, and she vanished from Tamino's sight. As daylight returned, poor Papageno came running to beg for Tamino's help.

"Hm, hm, hm, hm," mumbled Papageno.

Tamino could not break the golden padlock. But at last the three ladies agreed to set the bird-catcher free.

They gave a
golden flute with
magic powers to
the Prince, and to
Papageno some magical bells. Together they
would go to Sarastro's castle.

"Three gentle spirits shall protect and
guide you," the ladies promised Tamino as they
said farewell.

So when they reached Sarastro's domain,
Tamino was watched over by the three spirits.

But Papageno wandered off into the castle. He
looked into a splendid hall — and there sat a
young girl, pale and still! Papageno went near.
Suddenly he came face to face with a man
in a purple turban. Each was terrified by the other.

"A devil!" shrieked Papageno.

"A devil!" shrieked the turbaned man, and
they both ran away.

The man, who was called Monostatos, was Pamina's cruel guard. Papageno took courage at his flight.

"I've never feared even the strangest bird," he said to himself. "Why should I be afraid of him?"

Once again he approached the girl. He told her that her mother had sent a young Prince to rescue her and that the Prince already loved her. At the thought of how brave he was for her sake, Pamina immediately fell in love with Tamino in return.

This made the little bird-catcher sad. "I wish *I* had a little Papagena to love!" he sighed.

Then he caught Pamina by the hand and they fled from the hall before Monostatos returned.

Meanwhile, the spirits aiding Tamino had led him
before the three doors of a splendid Temple. In
the central doorway appeared an ancient priest.

"What do you seek, intruder?" he
demanded.

"Truth and love," replied the Prince.

"Then you do well to come here," said the
priest. "But you can find neither truth nor love if
inspired by vengeance."

"Not even vengeance against the tyrant?"

"No tyrant lives here," said the priest
sternly.

"But is not this the domain of Sarastro?"

"Sarastro," said the priest, "is no cruel sorcerer. He protects Pamina from the evil influence of her mother, the Queen of Night. The girl's father has long been of the brotherhood of the Temple, and Pamina is alive and safe."

Overcome with joy, Tamino played his golden flute till the wild beasts of the forest gathered to listen.

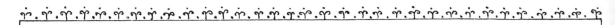

Then Tamino heard Papageno's pipe in the
distance.

"Perhaps Pamina is already found," he
thought, full of hope.

He blew a trill on his own flute, and
Papageno's pipe answered it.

They began to search for each other
through the wood.

But Monostatos was also in the wood with a group of slaves, searching for the runaways. Now he caught sight of them both. "Put them in chains!" he ordered the slaves.

Pamina was terrified. But Papageno, remembering the magic bells, shook them into music.

The slaves were so entranced that they dropped the chains and broke into a clumsy dance. One by one they danced away, singing to the lilting sound of the bells.

"Oh pretty sound! Oh lovely music! La la la, la la la!"

Over the tinkling bells came the sound of
trumpets. Voices cried: "Hail! All hail to Sarastro!"

Six great lions drew a chariot in solemn
procession. Down from it stepped Sarastro, and
Pamina threw herself at his feet.

"Forgive me!" she begged. "It was only
because of the unkindness of the wicked
Monastatos that I tried to escape."

Sarastro readily forgave her. But he would
not let her return to her mother.

"Speak of her no more," he commanded. "She is dark and deceitful, and would ruin your happiness."

Even as he spoke, Monostatos rushed in, dragging Tamino with him. When the young lovers saw each other for the first time, they embraced with joy. But Sarastro sternly separated them. He told Tamino that he must undergo great trials to prove himself worthy of the brotherhood of the Temple. Only then could he win Pamina.

The Prince was ready to venture anything for his beloved.

Monostatos had expected a reward for revealing the plot to rescue Pamina. Instead he was dismissed with the slaves and punished for his unkindness.

Resentful and malicious, he stole that night into the temple gardens where Pamina was sleeping. As he crept near her, full of cruel thoughts, a sudden clap of thunder frightened him. Out of the darkness came the Queen of Night.

"Begone, wicked man!" she commanded.

Pamina woke at her voice and cried out: "Mother! Mother!"

"Child, where is the Prince whom I sent to rescue you?"

"He too follows Sarastro."

"Alas then, you are lost unless you are strong. You must kill Sarastro."

She thrust a dagger into Pamina's hand, then faded again into the darkness, crying for vengeance.

Pamina stood horrified, holding the dagger. She heard the sound of the golden flute and fled towards it longing for Tamino's help and comfort.

But bitter was her grief when she found him. The Prince's first trial was a vow of silence. Already the Queen of Night's ladies had tempted him to break it, but he had resisted. So now he was silent before his Princess, and she went away weeping.

Poor Papageno was unhappy too. He was cold and lonely, hungry and thirsty. To comfort himself he played on his magic bells. If only he too could have a little wife, a sweetheart!

Just then he heard the tap of a stick, and an old
woman shuffled towards him, carrying a goblet.

"For me?" asked Papageno hopefully.

"For you, my angel."

Papageno drank thirstily. "How old are you,
grandmother?"

"Eighteen years and two minutes."

"Eighty years and two minutes?"

"*Eighteen* years and two minutes."

"And have *you* got a sweetheart?" asked
Papageno, astonished.

"To be sure I have, my darling."

"Is he as young as you are?"

"No, a little older."

"And what is his name?"

"Papageno."

"Papageno! I — *I* am your sweetheart?"

"Who else, my darling? Promise to marry me, or be imprisoned here forever."

Very reluctantly he gave his hand to the old woman. But at his touch she turned into a young girl dressed all in feathers, just like himself.

"Papagena!" he cried.

But she fled from him
into the darkness,
and he followed
blindly.

Pamina too was in despair. Her mother had left
her, her Prince had abandoned her. Desperately
she raised the dagger to plunge it into her own
heart.

"Stay! Stay, unhappy girl!"
The three gentle spirits
had come to help her.
"Tamino still loves you,"
they told her. "And love
will protect you and
overcome every danger."

They led her to join her Prince in the trials that lay before him. In front of them stood iron gates that led to two high mountains. From one of them poured terrible flames against a burning sky. Down the other, which reared into a black and stormy sky, roared a great waterfall.

Bravely the two lovers passed between the gates and walked through the fire, Tamino playing on his magic flute, and Pamina following close behind him.

Then they faced the dreadful waterfall but the
magic of the music brought them through to
safety. Trumpets and joyful song greeted them
from the Temple.

"Triumph, triumph, you noble pair! Your
courage has conquered. Enter the Temple's open
doors."

All this time Papageno wandered in despair,
crying out in grief for his lost sweetheart.

"Papagena! Papagena! Papagena! Have I
lost you for ever?"

He had found a rope and thought he would
hang himself, but he was a little afraid! "I'll just
count three first," he said. "One, two …"

"No," cried the gentle spirits, coming
swiftly to his aid. "Foolish Papageno! Why don't
you sound your magic bells?"

He had quite forgotten
his bells. But as he shook
them, Papagena came running
to meet him.

They broke into a dance
of joy, hopping lightly round
each other like happy
birds.

As they danced they sang to each other.

     "Pa – pa – pa – pa – pa – Papagena!"

     "Pa – pa – pa – pa – pa – Papageno!"

     "Mine for ever!" "Yours for ever!"

     "My little wife!" "My little husband!"

     "We shall have so many little birds –"

     "First a little Papageno –"

     "Then a little Papagena –"

     "Then another Papageno!" "Then another Papagena!"

     "So many Papagenos …" "So many Papagenas … shall bless our nest."

While the bird-catcher and his little wife sang to
each other, night lingered over the Temple. Up the
great staircase crept Monostatos, beckoning the
Queen and her ladies to follow, in a last desperate
attempt to defeat Sarastro.

But light streamed suddenly through the
doorway above, revealing Sarastro in all his
majesty.

Thunder rolled and lightning split the sky.

"Oh, oh!" cried the Queen. "Our power is broken! We are cast into eternal night!"

Dark clouds swirled down to engulf her with her companions. They vanished for ever, defeated by the power of light.

Now all the Temple shone beneath its brilliance and the priests gathered around Sarastro.

The three gentle spirits brought garlands of
flowers for Tamino and Pamina, who were united
with much joy, while a great hymn of praise hailed
the triumph of light over darkness.